Become

Be Who God Has Called You to Be
Come into His Presence and Become More
Than You Ever Thought Was Possible

ELLEN VANDA

WESTBOW®
PRESS
A DIVISION OF THOMAS NELSON
& ZONDERVAN

Scripture taken from the New King James Version®. Copyright
© 1982 by Thomas Nelson. Used by permission.

Scripture taken from The Voice ™. Copyright © 2006, 2007, 2008 by
Ecclesia Bible Society. Used by permissions. All rights reserved.

All scripture quotations, unless otherwise indicated, are taken from
the Holy Bible, New International Version®, NIV®. Copyright
©1973, 1978, 1984, 2011 by Biblica, Inc.™ Used by permission of
Zondervan. All rights reserved worldwide. www.zondervan.com The
"NIV" and "New International Version" are trademarks registered in
the United States Patent and Trademark Office by Biblica, Inc.™

WestBow Press books may be ordered through booksellers or by contacting:

WestBow Press
A Division of Thomas Nelson & Zondervan
1663 Liberty Drive
Bloomington, IN 47403
www.westbowpress.com
1 (866) 928-1240

Because of the dynamic nature of the Internet, any web addresses or
links contained in this book may have changed since publication and
may no longer be valid. The views expressed in this work are solely those
of the author and do not necessarily reflect the views of the publisher,
and the publisher hereby disclaims any responsibility for them.

Certain stock imagery © Thinkstock.

ISBN: 978-1-4908-3055-1 (sc)
ISBN: 978-1-4908-3054-4 (hc)
ISBN: 978-1-4908-3056-8 (e)

Printed in the United States of America.

Library of Congress Control Number: 2014904853

WestBow Press rev. date: 4/1/2014

Contents

Introduction

As I started writing this book, I remember the intimidation of a blank page......so much room to write. Where do I begin? Thus, my blank page begins here, with God as my co-author.

I have to admit that I enjoy writing, but have never had time to sit down and even consider writing a book...besides, what could I possibly be the subject matter expert on? What could I say that would encourage women to take time out of their busy life to want to read my book? I have been lost in the corporate world for so many years while juggling housework, laundry, bills, gardening...where does writing a book come in? Lord, are you sure you want to use me in this way? Lord, wouldn't the obvious be to use my husband and me in music ministry? *BUT GOD* had a plan!

It all began at the Women of Faith Conference in Peoria, IL the weekend of August 16, 2013.This event was truly the only women's activity that I have ever attended. So let me share how it all came to be, it is an amazing story and blessing from God.

On a Sunday morning in June, the church we attended showed a video announcing the Women of Faith conference that was coming to our area. It shared clips of the speakers, groups, etc. that would be part of the conference team. God began tugging at my heart to attend the conference. After church I spoke with the pastor's wife who indicated that she had only ten remaining tickets to sell for the event. I discussed it with my husband. He thought it was a great idea and wanted me to make plans to attend. I wanted to go but was concerned about spending the money after recently losing my job.

For several weeks I thought about it, as the tugging at my heart continued. I finally circled back with the pastor's wife regarding the tickets, only to find that they had all been purchased for her group. I resolved to make attending the conference the following year a priority; *BUT GOD* had another plan.

The week of the conference I received an email from the pastor's wife indicating that a dear friend and part of their extended family had passed away, and she would not be able to attend the conference. While she was needing to find her replacement, my name came up in conversation with another woman from the church. They discussed how I had wanted to go, but missed the timely opportunity. Remembering this, she reached out to me to see if I was still interested in attending, before sending out an email to the congregation.

Being presented with the opportunity to attend the conference in her place was a blessing in itself, then she offered her ticket to me at half price! While reading her email, my eyes filled with tears flowing down my face and on to the computer. I realized that God wanted me to attend this conference, and *He* made a way for me to go. We serve an amazing God who knows the desires of our hearts and always shows up just in time.

The conference was awesome. Over five thousand women gathered together to fellowship, praise and worship God; it was an incredible experience. During the weekend event we found ourselves laughing and crying together, bonding with complete strangers, while God ministered to us in a way that only *He* could do.

The first night of the conference I knew God was revealing certain things to me, and I felt the Holy Spirit impressing upon me to pay close attention and to take it all in. At times during the weekend, I would find myself questioning exactly what I was led to observe; I didn't want to miss any part of God's direction. I carefully watched the praise teams, the worship leaders, the communicators and videos. I found myself taking notes throughout the event. Whatever God was up to, I wanted to make sure I didn't miss out and that I had my part covered.

Sunday morning finally arrived, I remember being so thrilled to sit beside my husband at church, worshipping the Lord together. I definitely missed him during the worship at the conference, it just wasn't the same without him by my side.

While the pastor was delivering the morning sermon, God began to flood my mind with thoughts, sentences, definitions and scriptures, directing me to write them down. After taking notes all weekend, one would think that I understood the process and came to the service prepared; however, that would be an incorrect assumption. I did not. I reached for the only paper that I had, my church bulletin. Quickly I started writing everything that the Lord was laying on my heart. After thinking I had captured the words that He was giving me, I quietly placed everything back where it belonged on the pew.

A few moments later, God began giving me more things to write down, so I collected my bulletin and pen, and continued to fill the borders. This went on throughout the entire sermon. I am pretty certain the pastor thought I was really getting excited from his sermon, as he would occasionally look down and smile, acknowledging my note taking.

In church, my husband and I always sit on the second row during services to avoid distractions. On this particular Sunday morning, *I was* the distraction. Several times I found myself putting my bulletin and pen down only to pick them up again. I remember thinking to myself, surely others are noticing all of this, as I tried to conceal my overwhelming excitement. I remember there were times when it seemed that I couldn't write fast enough to capture everything God was giving me; the information flowed so freely. I was completely awestruck… the anointing was falling on me and the presence of God was amazing. These were moments that I will never forget and will always cherish.

While writing as quickly as I could, trying desperately not to miss one phrase, my handwriting was everything short of legible. Looking up at my husband to get his attention, I moved the bulletin over towards him so he could see what was happening. He looked down, smiled, and shook his head. I am getting an incredible revelation from God and he shook his head. Yes he did. It took everything I had to refrain from whispering in his ear in efforts to share what was happening… until he shook his head, then I figured he could just wait.

At one point I remember asking the Lord, "What is all of this that I am writing? What does it mean?" Then the He answered, "We are writing a book." Once again, I struggled to hold back the tears. I was completely overwhelmed by the presence of God.

As the sermon closed, I heard the small still voice of God telling me the book should be titled, "Become". I hesitated to write this down, trying to recall if I had seen other books with the same name. Obviously noticing my hesitation, and being the God that *He is*…*He* gave me a clear vision of the front of the book, how it was to be laid out and what it meant. WOW, you can't ask for more clarity than that, so here it is ladies…

Be Come.

Be Who God has called you to be
Come into His presence
And you will **Become** more than you ever thought was possible.

Please note, scriptures referenced in this book are taken from the New International Version of the Bible unless otherwise indicated.

Chapter One

Be Ready for Change, Fasten your Seatbelt!

When you ask God to use you, be ready for everything to change. I have learned that God does not always use you in the obvious ways; what you may be experienced in, what you are familiar with, or within your talent arena. He may require you to step out of your comfort zone and embark in unchartered territories. Just when you think you have it all figured out – how God is going to use you, how you can serve Him and advance His kingdom….God tells you what *He* desires, and what *He* really wants you to do.

A few months ago I found myself in unchartered territory with little understanding as to how God could use a sudden tornado in my life to move me to a deeper relationship with and understanding of Him. Here's my story.

It was a Monday morning. Of course it was. Funny how those in the working world dread Monday's. I am not sure which is worse going to the dentist or facing a Monday morning at the office. On this particular Monday morning, I had just finished a meeting with my team, getting everyone geared for the week ahead, when I heard someone in the front office. To my amazement, I was soon introduced to a woman who worked for the same company. I was caught off guard, as no one from the corporate office, or the other branches had ever been to our office. I had worked for this company for a year and had never met anyone, including the CEO whom I reported to directly.

Her visit was unannounced and unexpected, which in corporate terms indicates trouble. She entered my office and explained that she was there to train one of the members of my team- a clear indication of the day I was about to have. The team did not understand the need for her visit and were very uncomfortable with her presence as she was quite disingenuous throughout the day. As the manager, it was my responsibility to assure the team that everything was fine and I asked them to carry on with their usual responsibilities.

It was a very long day. God had revealed to me early on that she was there to end my employment. At one point during the day I knew I needed to spend time with the Lord. I needed to feel His warm embrace, and hear Him tell me that everything was going to be okay. I found my quiet place in the women's bathroom. There, I found myself in the presence of God, even in such a lowly place. That's how Jesus came into this world- in a lowly place- and that is where God's finest work is completed, when we have met defeat. God shows up on the scene triumphant, providing assurance, comfort, and peace while standing beside His children, regardless of their geographical location.

The end of the day finally came, I assured my team that everything would be okay and to go home. After they had left, the woman indicated that we needed to call a gentleman from corporate who also assisted the team. Once we connected with him, he proceeded to tell me that he wanted to deliver the news in person but he was 110 miles away, and hated doing it this way. He thanked me for all of my hard work, wanted me to know it was appreciated, and then told me that they were taking the account that I managed in a different direction, and that my journey with the company ended there. I smiled, thanked them both for the opportunity, and began gathering my personal belongings.

In the midst of this sudden storm in my life, I felt the calm assurance that God was setting me free from a world in which I did not belong. I felt a peace beyond comprehension and knew that God was in control. I had just lost a very good paying job with generous benefits, and yet I was smiling and very calm, assuring the woman who was following me around that everything was going to be fine.

She stood over me as I gathered my things. Needing to be watched was humiliating. I was the one who found the office, set it up, decorated it and built the team and the account, and now I was being closely monitored. But I was smiling and found myself laughing inside. A time that should have brought me to tears brought joy because of God's awesome presence.

God is with us even in the fiery furnace, just as He was with Shadrach, Meshach, and Abednego. The flames will not harm us, as we are dancing in the fire with our Lord and Savior! The children of Israel faced many trials and obstacles when they were freed from Egypt, but GOD always showed up and delivered them in their time of need. I have come to realize that even when we face the Red Sea of our lives, when we think we are going under, and may even drown, God will not let the waters sweep over His children.

> When you pass through the waters, I will be with you; And when you pass through the rivers, they will not sweep over you. When you walk through the fire, you will not be burned; The flames will not set you ablaze. (Isaiah 43:2)

As I drove out of the parking garage, I called my husband, Eric, to let him know that I was on my way home. Earlier, as the day unfolded, I texted him to be in prayer, making him aware of the events that were taking place. Later, I also texted him that I had been terminated, was packing up my belongings, and would reach out to him when I was on my way home.

When Eric answered the phone, it was very hard for me not to cry, all the emotions that had been building all day were longing to be released in a flood of tears. Then he said, "Baby, God just told me that you would be calling, and I was to tell you that *He* has set you free." All I could say was, "I know *He* has set me free". But free from what and for what I had yet to understand.

My mother has always said: "Anyone that thinks living the Christian life is dull and boring has no idea what they have in store for them. God is anything but boring and predictable." Isn't that the truth? Just when we think our lives are on the corporate merry-go-round, destined for promotions, stress, endless work weeks, unrelenting deadlines, and, of course benefits that will enable us to get medical attention as a part of the aforementioned perks of Corporate America, God shows up with a Plan.

God's ways are more creative, complex, and mysterious than we can ever begin to imagine. God has known from the moment we were created what His plans are for our lives. This is an obvious time to share one of my favorite scriptures: "'For I know the plans I have for you,' declares the Lord, 'plans to prosper you and not to harm you, plans to give you hope and a future.'" (Jeremiah 29:11)

He allows the world to shake us up and do its best to break us so He can restore us and make us stronger than we ever thought possible for His purpose. Amazing how God always goes before us and makes the crooked places straight.

> I will go before thee, and make the crooked places straight. I will break in pieces the gates of brass, and cut in sunder the bars of iron: And I will give thee the treasures of darkness, and hidden riches of secret places, that thou mayest know that I, the Lord, which call thee by thy name, am the God of Israel. (Isaiah 45: 2-3 KJV)

The NIV translation of this scripture tells us that God will level the mountains that stand in His way for us. What a powerful and amazing God we serve.

> I will go before you and will level the mountains; I will break down gates of bronze and cut through bars of iron. I will give you the treasures of darkness, riches stored in secret places, so that you may know that I am the Lord, the God of Israel, who summons you by name.

So, here I am with a career that was right on target, launched into the depths of unemployment. Anyone who has ever been there understands what I am writing about. I have never been one to assume it could never happen to me, as I have spent too many years working in the staffing industry, which could be another book of its own. Unemployment is a benefit that you appreciate when you realize the severance pay is over, and is not coming back. The electronic deposit that you have come to expect in your bank account is no longer there, but is replaced with a third of what you brought home every week. *But God* is greater than unemployment and severance pay; He always provides for His children. He has a plan, and this book is part of His unending love for you and me.

He is making a way for this child of His to reach out and touch the hearts of women like you. God is using this time in my life for His glory, and I stand in amazement at what He is giving me to share with you. I am blessed beyond any comprehension to think that God could use me with all of my inadequacies and limitations, to share His love for you.

When you begin asking God to use you for His glory, your life will change. Every expectation you may have as to how things will play out may never turn out the way that you had planned. God has sent me to tell you that it will turn out the way that God has always planned, for He knew your destiny and your purpose before you were even born.

> Before I formed you in the womb I knew you, Before you were born I set you apart; I appointed you as a prophet to the nations. (Jeremiah 1:5)

I've shared the reality of how this book began to help us understand that God isn't defined by our expectations. He is not constrained by our inadequacies and limitations. He is God and He has a plan for each of us. He will guide and direct our paths, leading us where He had planned for us to be all along.

Chapter Two

Becoming

Becoming is a journey that is unique for each one of us. God has a plan, a purpose, a destiny designed exclusively for you. His fingerprints are visible in every part of your life. Have you ever noticed them? Have you looked in the mirror to admire God's work? How exciting it is to think that the same God who created the universe, is up to something just as big in your life. Why do I say it's big? Have you ever known God to do anything small? The greatest part of this adventure is knowing that you are not in it alone, He is there every step of the way.

> I can do all things through Christ who strengthens me. (Philippians 4:13 NKJV)

Becoming is not something that we have to do alone, we have a Savior, a friend who is closer than a brother / sister (Proverbs 18). There is only one person that can prevent you from becoming the woman God is calling you to be….and that is YOU.

What holds us back from becoming who God has created us to be?

Comparison

Growing up I was blessed to have a mother and father who served the Lord, raised their children in the church, and introduced us to Jesus at a very young age. My parents led by example, showing us the true meaning of being a Christian. They taught us about God's unconditional love, His mercy and grace.

In the church I was blessed to have the influence of many Godly women whose faith simply amazed me. I remember the women who served faithfully in the kitchen. They never grew weary of preparing meals for the congregation, camp meetings, funeral dinners and also serving those who were "home bound" and unable to cook.

I remember the grandmothers and mothers who spent hours on their knees praying and seeking God for their children, family, friends, leaders and nation. After every service I watched them walk to the alter, kneeling down on their knees, crying out to God to meet the needs in people's lives. Prayer warriors who lovingly wrapped their arms around others who were facing difficult situations, praying with them, holding them as they cried.

I remember the Sunday school teachers who faithfully gave of their time to teach children about God's love. Women who left their fingerprint on children's hearts and childhood memories. Special ladies who made such a difference in my life. When I became a teenager, I referred to these women as the "Proverbs women."

My mother worked during most of my childhood and teenage years, leaving her very little time to serve in church; however, she always did as much as she could do. Mom and I used to talk about "The Proverbs Women", and how neither of us felt we would ever be able to fill those shoes. It was a subject that always made us laugh after comparing ourselves to the list of our most admired women. It was funny how our list would always include the same names, precious women of God that will never be forgotten.

Perhaps you have had the same thoughts while you were growing up, never quite measuring up to the "Proverbs Women". Maybe you find yourself juggling between marriage, children and career and cannot begin to fit a *Proverbs Woman* job description on your resume. The *ideal Godly woman* is something that you simply cannot begin to compare yourself with. *This* is your first mistake….you need to stop comparing yourself to others. God has a unique plan for your life.

The Proverbs 31 Woman is someone of strong character, who is wise and skillful with her resources. She is a woman of great compassion. Believe it or not she is a career woman, working in her home or career as unto the Lord. She is not defined by her achievements. Her accomplishments arise as a result of her relationship with God, giving Him the glory in all that she does.

The Proverbs Woman is not a domestic woman who creates the most incredible meals and maintains an immaculate home every hour of the day. Her beauty is not defined by the line of make-up she wears, nor the designer labels she clothes herself with. Her worth is not determined by where she shops or how much money she has in the bank.

The Proverbs 31 Woman is a woman, like yourself, who is totally sold out to God! She is merely an inspiration, not an expectation. Let me repeat this one more time. The Proverbs 31 Woman is an inspiration, not an expectation. Whew! I don't know about you, but this just released years of frustration, stress and pressure from my life! For so long, I have used Proverbs 31 as my God meter and spiritual measuring stick. Always missing the mark that I was aiming for. For so long I have found myself longing to be more like the Proverbs Woman, only to find out that I have been all along! Wow, I feel like I just received a promotion!

When you stop comparing yourself to others and begin to align your life with God's direction and His purpose, you will be amazed how He will use you for His kingdom! Jesus gave up His life for you, He loved you all the way to the cross. You don't have to *qualify* for this gift, it has already been given to you. All that you must do is open your heart to Him, receive his love, His mercy and forgiveness. His grace covers the difference between who we are and the excellence of the Proverbs Woman.

Condemnation

In Romans 8:1-2 we find a familiar verse that many of us know, yet somehow forget when the enemy reminds us of our failures, defeat, past mistakes and sinful nature. "Therefore, there is now no condemnation for those who are in Christ Jesus, because through Christ Jesus the law of the Spirit of life set me free from the law of sin and death."

Sometimes we tend to be our own worst enemy when it comes to condemnation. We are so willing to believe that we are unworthy of God's forgiveness, His mercy and grace. We believe the lies of the enemy and others who may judge us. We need to start believing in what the Bible tells us about our past failures, sins and mistakes. John tells us that God is greater than what our heart may use to condemn us.

> Dear children, let us not love with words or tongue but with actions and in truth. 19 This then is how we know that we belong to the truth, and how we set our

hearts at rest in His presence, 20 whenever our hearts condemn us. For God is greater than our hearts, and He knows everything. (I John 3:18-20)

Immediately following this verse, John tells us that if we do not allow our hearts to condemn us, we can receive anything we ask from God.

Dear friends, if our hearts do not condemn us, we have confidence before God and receive from Him anything we ask, because we obey His commands and do what pleases Him. (I John 3: 21-22)

If we desire to become what God has called us to be in Him, we have to leave condemnation at the feet of Jesus, forgiving ourselves as Christ has forgiven us. There is no one in your life that is able to place you under condemnation when you are a child of the Living God. *He* has saved you, forgiven you, and set you free from all condemnation and clothed you in a robe of righteousness. Paul teaches us about *righteousness* in Romans chapter 3.

But now a righteousness from God, apart from law, has been made known, to which the Law and the Prophets testify. This righteousness from God comes through faith in Jesus Christ to all who believe. There is no difference, for all have sinned and fall short of the glory of God, and are justified freely by His grace

through the redemption that came by Christ Jesus.
(Romans 3: 21-24)

In your journey of *Becoming* with God, lay down the baggage.
Forgive yourself, learn from your failures, mistakes and bad
decisions. Chalk it up to experience. God has given you a clean
slate to begin writing on. Use it to write about the new chapters
of your life, as you seek to become more like Him.

Remember…Your Past is in The Past

Have you ever gotten in your car to go somewhere and put it in
reverse by mistake? Suddenly you realize that you are heading
in the wrong direction as your car begins to move backwards.
Many of us try to live our lives in this manner, always moving
backwards instead of living forward. If we insist in keeping our
lives in reverse, we will never experience the journey that God
has placed directly in front of us.

Paul teaches us in Philippians chapter 3 about pressing on to the
goal that Christ has for each and every one of us.

> Not that I have already obtained all this, or have already
> been made perfect, but I press on to take hold of that
> for which Christ Jesus took hold of me. Brothers, I do
> not consider myself yet to have taken hold of it. But
> one thing I do: Forgetting what is behind and straining

toward what is ahead, I press on toward the goal to win the prize for which God has called me heavenward in Christ Jesus. (Philippians 3: 12–14)

In chapter 43 of Isaiah, God tells the people of Israel through His prophet Isaiah that He is doing something new. He asks them to forget the former things, stop dwelling on the past and start looking at what is springing up. I believe God is still telling us the same words today. He has so much He wants to do through us; however, we must be willing to leave our pasts behind us and press towards the goal He has for us.

I understand what it is to have a past that I wish I could change. I would love to erase, the hind-site lessons proven true time after time. I am here to tell you that Jesus has erased your past. He has given you the gift of forgiveness and all you have to do is accept His gift of salvation. Once you have accepted His gift, it is time to start living forward and experiencing God's plan for your life. We all have many miles ahead of us and we will never get there living our lives in reverse!

Procrastination

I hesitate to include this word in a book written for women. I thought this was a word that was always used when referring to the male gender. Believe it or not ladies, we are just as guilty of procrastinating as the male species.

Think about the days that never contain enough hours within them. The day you were certain someone pranked you by moving the clock forward several hours. The day you were pretty sure ended before you ever got started. The day that you could not possibly fit one more thing into your schedule, even if it meant spending time with the Lord. We have all been there, and some of us are still there. Daily we try to accomplish everything on our list, only to find that it wouldn't fit into a twenty four hour window, regardless of our level of organization.

I have discovered one truth that is helping me spend more time with God and I want to share this with you. The concept is very simple. *If you wait to spend time with God, when you have time to spend, you will never have enough time.* The enemy will create enough distractions to make sure of it.

When you continue to procrastinate spending time with God, you will soon you will realize that you have created a new habit. Habits are a part of who we are, a result of our priorities and lifestyle. I challenge you today to make a decision to spend time with God. Make *Him* the priority in your life.

So many of us have misconceptions of what spending time with God should be. I struggled with this as well until I began including Him in all parts of my day. I sing songs of praise to Him while I am in the shower. I talk with Him while I am putting on my make-up and getting ready for the day. I spend time singing and talking with Him during my morning commute, while listening to my favorite worship songs. Before I enter my workplace, a conference room or participate in a conference call, I always ask Him to go before me. If my day gets completely out of control, I sneak away and find a spot to spend a few minutes with Him in prayer. At the end of my workday, we spend time together during the commute home. I absolutely love spending time in His presence minutes before falling to sleep, praying and listening.

Our relationship with the Lord is just like any other relationship; the more we put into it, the more we will get out of it. God is waiting to hear from you. He wants to help you, encourage you, lift your burdens, direct your life, and just spend time with you. He created you to have fellowship with Him.

I hope that you are encouraged and have found strength through God's Word and this chapter to start pressing forward to become the woman *He* has called you to be. Through God you are able to overcome whatever obstacles that may be in your path. Start living forward, put your life in drive and begin to enjoy the ride like you never have before. The book of Revelations contains a great promise for those who *overcome*.

> I am coming soon. Hold on to what you have, so that no one will take your crown. Him who overcomes I will make a pillar in the temple of my God. Never

again will he leave it. I will write on him the name of my God and the name of the city of my God, the new Jerusalem, which is coming down out of heaven from my God; and I will also write on him my new name. (Revelations 3:11–12)

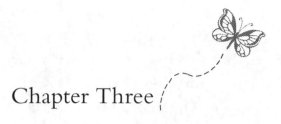

Chapter Three

The "Be" Attitudes

During the Sermon on the Mount, as recorded in Matthew chapter five, Jesus begins teaching those who gathered, introducing what we know as "The Beatitudes".

> Blessed are the poor in spirit, for theirs is the kingdom of heaven. Blessed are those who mourn, for they will be comforted. Blessed are the meek, for they will inherit the earth. Blessed are those who hunger and thirst for righteousness, for they will be filled.

Blessed are the merciful, for they will be shown mercy. Blessed are the pure in heart, for they will see God. Blessed are the peacemakers, for they will be called sons of God. Blessed are those who are persecuted because of righteousness, for theirs is the kingdom of heaven. Blessed are you when people insult you, persecute you and falsely say all kinds of evil against you because of me. Rejoice and be glad, because great is your reward in heaven, for in the same way they persecuted the prophets who were before you. (Matthew 5:3-12)

Jesus uses this opportunity to teach the disciples and those who gathered how to be more like Him, so they may be blessed by God's rewards in heaven. In the corporate world we would call this Jesus' Organizational Alignment Methodology, the organizational chart of heaven. The last in this world, those who are overlooked by our society, will be first in the kingdom of heaven, as He teaches in Matthew chapter 20. Wealth, power and authority are of little value in heaven.

The most effective way to reach others is by being a living example of Jesus Christ. In the Bible, God's Holy Word, we are given the *instruction manual for the Christian life*. As you take time to study the Bible, you will be amazed how the Word penetrates your heart. The pages come alive in your mind while the words speak to and nourish your soul.

In Romans, Paul continues our instruction manual for the Christian life by adding *How to be a Living Sacrifice for the Lord*.

> Love must be sincere. Hate what is evil; cling to what is good. Be devoted to one another in brotherly love. Honor one another above yourselves. Never be lacking in zeal, but keep your spiritual fervor, serving the Lord. Be joyful in hope, patient in affliction, faithful in prayer. Share with God's people who are in need. Practice hospitality. Bless those who persecute you; bless and do not curse. Rejoice with those who rejoice; mourn with those who mourn. Live in harmony with one

another. Do not be proud, but be willing to associate with people of low position. Do not be conceited. Do not repay anyone evil for evil. Be careful to do what is right in the eyes of everyone. If it is possible, as far as it depends on you, live at peace with everyone. Do not take revenge, my friends, but leave room for God's wrath, for it is written: "It is mine to avenge; I will repay," says the Lord. On the contrary: "If your enemy is hungry, feed him; if he is thirsty, give him something to drink. In doing this, you will heap burning coals on his head." Do not be overcome by evil, but overcome evil with good. (Romans 12: 9-21)

Allow me to introduce you to the *Be Attitudes. The Instruction Manual on How to Behave.*

Be of true, sincere love to one another.

Sincere, genuine love for one another requires effort. Genuine love is contagious, and will spread like fire. It will touch people's lives. Everyone wants to be loved. Some people are sponges, waiting to soak up any form of love. They have seen so many failed examples, they long to be loved unconditionally. Carry God's unconditional love to the world so that people may come to know what true love really is. Show others the love that God showed us when He sacrificed His Son on the cross to purchase our salvation.

Be certain to avoid and hate what is evil, clinging to what is good.

Paul teaches us in Philippians to use our mind to think about things that are pleasing to God.

> Finally, brothers, whatever is true, whatever is noble, whatever is right, whatever is pure, whatever is lovely, whatever is admirable--if anything is excellent or praiseworthy--think about such things. Whatever you have learned or received or heard from me, or seen in me-put into practice. And the God of peace will be with you. (Philippians 4:8-9)

In the New Testament we are given are simple instruction concerning evil.

> Test everything. Hold on to the good. Avoid every kind of evil. (I Thessalonians 5:21)

This portion of scripture encourages us to check our spiritual meter when we encounter anything that may not be of God. We need to get into God's word, find out what He tells us about a situation or the circumstances that we find ourselves in. We live in an evil society that does not have our best interests at heart. Satan uses half-truths to misguide us and distract us from the path that God has placed us on.

Start each day by asking God for directions for your day; ask Him to help you fix your mind on Him, and to guide you away from any evil doing that crosses your path.

Be devoted to one another in brotherly (sisterly) love, honoring one another above yourself.

Loving one another seems to be a natural effort for most Christians, we have been given a great example to follow. When it comes to putting others above ourselves is where it gets tricky. As my daddy used to say, "That's where the rubber meets the pavement," a phrase he would use to get right to the point, or *heart of the action.*

In Romans, Paul is calling us to show respect for our brothers and sisters in Christ. Guarding their reputations as if they were your own. It is a privilege to put other's needs before our own needs, so that God can be glorified through our obedience. We should be devoted and eager to serve one another without hidden agendas or a motive for personal gain. Loving others more than we love ourselves, placing their needs before our own *is* the heart of the action.

Be full of zeal.

Paul tells us to "never be lacking in zeal, but to keep up your spiritual fervor, serving the Lord". Fervor simply means showing great intensity in spirit. Fervor is having excitement and enthusiasm for what God is doing in your life, in your home, in your church. If you find yourself as a "bench-warmer", watching from the sidelines…it is time to get in the game! Living for God is not a spectator sport. Get excited for what God is doing *and is* going to do in your life as you draw closer to Him.

The world is watching us, wanting to see if we are living what we believe. Are we walking the life we are talking about? It's time to dust off those pom-poms, wiggle into that cheerleading uniform and begin getting excited for our God! Start showing the same excitement we have at our son's baseball games, or our daughter's dance recital….

Stand up and be a megaphone shouting the praises of our *Awesome God*. If you have read the last chapter of the Bible, you know we are on the winning team. It's time to start showing it. Let's get excited!

Be joyful in hope.

Jesus came to earth from his heavenly home to give hope to a dying world. So many times during His ministry Jesus gave hope to the hurting, the broken, the lame, the deaf, the outcasts, and to the families who lost their loved ones. Telling them not to be afraid, but to believe in the One who sent Him.

Jesus teaches us in John chapter 16 that in this world we will have trouble, but to take heart, for *He* has overcome the world.

He is our hope. We must simply believe and put our hope and faith in Him.

In the last chapter and verse of Revelations the following words of hope are written, "The grace of the Lord Jesus be with God's people. Amen." The very last verse of the Bible is so encouraging. It gives us not only a promise, but a simple truth. We have the grace of our Lord Jesus with us, the hope of all generations. Be joyful in the hope that God has given us through His son, Jesus Christ.

Be patient in affliction.

David, a man after God's heart wrote in Psalms the following verse.

> I waited patiently for the Lord; He turned to me and heard my cry. He lifted me out of the slimy pit, out of the mud and mire; he set my feet on a rock and gave me a firm place to stand. He put a new song in my mouth, a hymn of praise to our God. Many will see and fear and put their trust in the Lord. (Psalm 40:1-3)

As David waited on the Lord, God was faithful; He lifted David from a pit of despair, setting his feet on a rock, providing him a firm place to stand. As David was being delivered, set free, God put a new song of praise in his mouth. Why did God do all of this? Because He knew many would watch

David's struggle through affliction and learn to put their trust in the Lord. David's despair brought glory to God as he waited patiently for God to respond.

Have you ever noticed how unbelievers watch carefully when we are faced with the loss of a job, death of a family member, divorce, financial devastation, turned down for a promotion, or any other adversity that we experience? The world sits by the sidelines to see if we really believe what we say we believe, awaiting our reaction to adversity. They want to know if our God is truly the faithful One that we have told them about. Does He really care for those who place their hope in Him?

God allows His children to go through pain, affliction, loss and trials that we struggle to understand for a reason. So *He will be glorified and exalted* when we are delivered. God is faithful and He will never forsake you in your time of need! God will deliver you. You can safely place your hope and trust in Him and know that He is there for you.

Be faithful in prayer.

For most of my life I have been lost in the concept of praying properly. I remember thinking that my prayers never measured up to others who would pray in church. Have you ever felt that the words in your prayers were not "spiritual" enough, not politically correct? That despite your efforts, you were unable to pray for things in the right manner? This is how I felt for a very long time, and was uncomfortable praying for others out loud. When I prayed silently, or at home, I knew that God understood what I was trying to say and was very forgiving for my lack of word choice.

One day I finally received my epiphany from the Lord. He wasn't sitting up there waiting to hear my eloquent words, He was simply waiting to hear from me. God desires for you to pull up a chair and talk to Him about your day, your concerns, your broken heart, your struggles, your needs and your dreams. He longs for you to talk with Him throughout your day. He wants to walk with you through the garden, accompany you during your bike ride, and walk with you beside the ocean as you listen to His marvelous handiwork. He wants to meet you in the ladies room when the end of your job has come, or when the world comes crashing down around you. He wants a relationship with you and the best way to build any relationship is communication. Prayer is simply a conversation with God, the Master of the universe, our Creator, our Savior, and very best friend.

My favorite time of the day is when I am taking my morning shower, and spending time with the Lord. I always say "Good Morning Father God", "Good Morning Jesus, my Savior and Friend", and "Good Morning Holy Spirit, you are welcome in my day." Every day we always take time to tell our husband, children and co-workers "good morning", why wouldn't we tell our Creator, Savior and Comforter the same? There is something about starting the day with God that makes everything easier as the day progresses.

God knows the desires of our hearts, He knows our needs before we even ask for His assistance. He is standing there with open arms and willing ears to hear from you…He wants to build a relationship with you; He wants to talk with you.

Be thoughtful and share with those who are in need.

Jesus called His twelve disciples from all types of occupations, lifestyles, and circumstances, asking them to follow Him. He invested His time in the disciples, teaching them more about God, the scriptures, and the *Great Commission*. He used parables to help them understand more about the Kingdom of God. He equipped them with the knowledge they would need to spread the gospel. Jesus gave them clear directions for their mission.

> As you go, preach this message: "The kingdom of heaven is near." Heal the sick, raise the dead, cleanse those who have leprosy, drive out demons. Freely you have received, freely give. (Matthew 10: 7-8)

In the second chapter of Acts, after Jesus was crucified, risen and transcended to heaven, the disciples carried out their mission. They began teaching and forming a fellowship of believers, giving to anyone who was in need, often times selling everything they had.

Today, our contributions may not be to sell everything that we own, but to give up something that is of great value, something that we never seem to have enough of, our time.

If God has given you a portion of wealth that you can give to bless others, "freely give". I know you have heard this said so many times but, often the testimonies that follow only confirm this concept over and over again. "You cannot out give God." As you begin to bless others with your time, money, or talent, God will pour His blessings into your life.

Be sure to practice hospitality.

> Above all, love each other deeply, because love covers over a multitude of sins. Offer hospitality to one another without grumbling. Each one should use whatever gift he has received to serve others, faithfully administering God's grace in its various forms. (I Peter 4:8-10)

Hospitality can best be defined as the practice of extending yourself to others in the direction of their need. For some, this could be a place to stay, for others a meal. For the single mother, it could mean helping her with childcare. For the homeless man it could be as simple as offering a meal and friendship. Letting him know that someone loves him and cares about what he is going through. Remember, you may be the only example of Jesus Christ these people will ever meet. What a great challenge and responsibility!

Be a blessing to those who persecute you.

> But I tell you: Love your enemies and pray for those who persecute you, that you may be sons of your Father in heaven. He causes his sun to rise on the evil and the good, and sends rain on the righteous and the unrighteous. If you love those who love you, what reward will you get? Are not even the tax collectors doing that? And if you greet only your brothers, what are you doing more than others? Do not even the pagans do that? Be perfect, therefore, as your heavenly Father is perfect. (Matthew 5: 44–48)

This is a tough one for most of us. We are called to love those who talk about us behind our back. Love the person who spread untruths about you around the office. Love those who laugh at your Christian faith. Love those who discriminate against you. Yes, this is what Jesus is telling us to do.

This is the time when prayer becomes our strong tower. It gives us strength and courage to love the unlovable people in our lives. As you begin to pray for those who persecute you, it not only changes your heart, but will change theirs as well. Whether they are Christians or unbelievers, prayer can tear down the walls surrounding their hearts. Prayer will unleash the Holy Spirit to begin working in their lives. For the unsaved, this could be the prayer that opens the door and introduces them to Jesus Christ. For the believer, this could be the prayer that breaks down the walls, destroying the chains that bind them. You may never have the opportunity to see the results of your prayer. But, you will live the victorious life that has promised for His children.

Be an encourager. Rejoice with those who rejoice. Mourn with those who mourn.

Numerous times, from the Old Testament through the New Testament, God tells us to encourage one another. We are to lift one another up during times of joy, sorrow, victory or defeat.

> Let us hold unswervingly to the hope we profess, for he who promised is faithful. And let us consider how we may spur one another on toward love and good deeds. Let us not give up meeting together, as some are in the habit of doing, but let us encourage one another – and all the more as you see the Day approaching. (Hebrews 10:23-25)

We are called to "spur" one another with encouragement, urging one another to continue the race that is in front of us. Do not give up. In the days ahead, things are going to get tough for the believer. As my mother used to tell me, "When the going gets tough, that's when the tough get going." Let us therefore "spur" one another and get going. We have a world to introduce to Jesus Christ!

Be deliberate to live in harmony with one another.

Being the music person that I am, when I hear the word "harmony", I think of notes that compose a harmonic sound. Tones that are so closely assembled, notes that are distinct yet different, all contributing to one beautiful sound. In a similar manner, this is what Paul is telling us to do.

Let's take a look at simple, triad chord. The first note illustrating of a group of believers who are closely woven to one another. The second note representing the unique talents, strengths and abilities that each member of this group has to offer. The third note emphasizing the unity that binds this group together. Composing a harmony that is precious to God's ear. The sound that is heard when His children come together, using their talents and spiritual gifts in one accord, living in unity with one another, as an act of worship to their Creator.

Be willing to associate with people in all walks of life, put away your pride. Do not be conceited.

Jesus reached out to people from all walks of life during His time here on this earth. He was baptized by a man who wore clothes made of camel hair, whose diet consisted of locusts and honey. He had dinner with tax collectors. He enjoyed his time on the water with the fishermen. Jesus hung out with Elijah and Moses on top of a mountain. He loved holding children in His arms. He met with the wealthy, healed the blind beggar and died on a cross between two thieves. Jesus loved everyone, He did not have a pride issue. The Son of God had every reason to be conceited, yet He was humble.

Paul asks us to put away our pride, and to begin seeing people as Jesus did. Every homeless beggar that we encounter is an opportunity to share the blessing that we all have been given, forgiveness and eternal life through Jesus Christ. Every little ragged, dirty, forgotten boy or girl is a child of the King of Kings. Every CEO of a company is going to meet the highest authority on all organizational charts one day, and needs to hear the truth about eternal life. Every person that we encounter during the course of our day is an opportunity to share the love of Jesus Christ. We may not always have the opportunity to speak with them, but we can offer a smile that shows them that we care and that there is a God in heaven who loves them.

Be convinced not to take revenge, but leave this is God's hands. Do not to repay anyone evil for evil.

As a child did you ever want to "get even" with someone who may have taken your bike, your doll, your jump rope or your best coloring book? What about those kids who just love to break your crayons. Ugh, you know what I mean, right? It's easy as a child to want to do the same thing that was done to you, repeat the behavior that hurt you so badly. You want to hear them cry and run to their mommy too, it's not cool to be the only one upset and sobbing hysterically.

Ellen Vanda

As adults, we sometimes find ourselves in this same situation. Hurt, broken, shamed, disrespected, used or being the topic of the conversation in the lunch room. Our first response should not be to retaliate or to get revenge. It should be an attitude of forgiveness.

I understand how hard this can be; I find it challenging at times as well. I have learned that if I can step out of the situation and immediately take it to the Lord in prayer, I receive immediate peace form God. He directs me in the ways of His righteousness and gives me a spirit of forgiveness.

Be consistent in doing right in the eyes of everyone, especially the Lord.

In Genesis chapter 13 we read the story of Abram and Lot who dwelled in the land that God provided for them to build a great nation. Abram and Lot both had significant wealth and livestock, which caused tension between their herdsmen, as they tried to share the land. Abram, in efforts to settle a dispute with his nephew, willingly gave Lot the first choice of the land and where he wanted his family to settle. Lot chose the well watered garden area of the Jordan, and settled in Sodom. Abram took the lesser of the land, making Canaan his new home. Lot's decision greatly reveals his character. He selected the best land for himself instead of considering the needs of his uncle. Lot's greed placed him in a city that was wicked and would eventually lead his family into temptation and destruction.

Abram showed a willingness to please God and do right in the eyes of his family. He understood that he had to settle the situation quickly as the quarreling between the two families would destroy both. Although he was older and entitled to the land of plenty, he took the initiative to bring peace into the families by allowing Lot to make the first choice. Abram wanted to do right in the eyes of God.

Be overcomers…overcome evil with good.

> Finally, be strong in the Lord and in His mighty power. Put on the full armor of God, so that you can take your stand against the devil's schemes. For our struggle is not against flesh and blood, but against the rulers, against the authorities, against the powers of this dark world and against the spiritual forces of evil in the heavenly realms. (Ephesians 6:10-12)

So many times in the Bible God tells us to be strong and courageous, standing firm in faith. Through His Son, Jesus Christ, we are overcomers. Jesus doesn't promise us that the road will always be easy. He doesn't promise us that we will never encounter the storms of life. However, He does promise us that He will never leave us or forsake us in our times of need.

> In this world you will have trouble. But take heart! I have overcome the world. (John 16: 33)

Be a vessel of peace, living in peace with everyone.

> Make every effort to live in peace with all men and to
> be holy; without holiness no one will see the Lord."
> (Hebrews 12:14)

Living in peace with one another simply means living without strife or discord. Our peace comes from knowing our Lord and Savior Jesus Christ. We need to understand that we serve the God who created this universe, and *He* has it all under control.

As we begin to practice the "Be Attitudes" that Paul shares with us in Romans, we will become more like Christ. Our lives will become a symphony which is precious to God's ears. Movements within the symphony that illustrate love, honor, zeal, joy, hope, patience, faithfulness, prayer, encouragement, sharing and caring. Music that glorifies our Heavenly Father and reflects His love for us. I encourage you to be a "Living Sacrifice", pointing the world to Jesus Christ through your love, actions, acceptance, forgiveness and encouragement to one another.

Chapter Four

Be Ready. It Will Happen to You.

Picture yourself at the mall standing in a department store. There in front of you is the purse you have admired, seeing it in so many magazines. Of course, you have to have it. The sales associate, noticing your interest, asks if there is anything she could show you. Without hesitation you ask her to bring the purse out of the glass cabinet. As she takes it out and places it on the counter you smell the fresh leather, such an inviting fragrance. You hold it, touch it, place it on your shoulder, see it in the mirror, and want it. You not only want it, you have to have it.

The sales associate asks if you will be using your store credit card. Immediately you recall this being the one that your husband said was no longer an option for you to use. The card that carries a balance as large as both of your monthly incomes combined. Yes, that one. Of course it is the only one in your wallet besides your debit card and checkbook.

You pause for a moment, and the enticement continues. You work so hard and contribute a significant salary to the household income. "You deserve it," continues to resonate in your head. Trying to capture a moment of rationality, you ask how much it will be. The associate explains the price tag is $399.00, which is a great price for this handbag.

Your first thought is, what a bargain, until your conscience begins to tell you that this purchase will most definitely max out your credit card. The one your husband asked you not to use. Property tax is due, as well as the homeowners insurance, school just started and Christmas is around the corner. "But you deserve it", the voice in your head is telling you. You realize that you are in quite the dilemma.

The sales person is needing to assist other customers, but is requiring an answer from you. In what seemed to be the worse timing for you, another customer approaches the counter and asks if that is the new bag shown in all the fashion magazines. The sales associate confirms that it is, and indicates that it is in such demand that they only received an initial shipment of just one. The one she is waiting for you to purchase.

Before you could give it a second thought, the plastic credit card jumped out of your purse and landed right in the hands of the associate. Wow that decision just made itself. What a relief. Besides, I deserve this.

As you walk away from the store you are trying to collect your thoughts on what just happened. The guilt begins to well up inside of you. Your hand closely holds the purchase that you are now regretting. Just as you begin to think about what you just did, the purse seems to come alive in your mind, asking you, "What are you waiting for? Don't you want to show me off to everyone at the mall?"

Once again, you think to yourself, I deserve this as you rush to the women's restroom to change out your handbag. Using the changing table, you quickly convert the old worn out handbag to the beautiful new purse. As you walk out of the bathroom, you turn to take one more glance at your purchase. Yes, you are looking good. Just the accessory you needed. While you finish your shopping, you notice others admiring your new purse. "They must be reading the same magazine," you think while quietly giggling to yourself. You feel great and are enjoying the simple pleasures of your career.

Now it's time to go home. You hope and pray that no one notices your new purse, at least not today. The feeling of remorse rises up inside of you, while your heartbeat seems louder than usual. Upon arriving at home, your husband comes to welcome you, asking if you enjoyed your afternoon. Looking into his eyes, you suddenly are not so proud of the new bag. You know how the rest of the story goes, it always ends the same way. Temptation has a large price tag.

I tell you this story as everyone can relate to it in one manner or another, we have all been there. Our decisions and conclusions may be different; however, the emotions and thoughts are somewhat similar. Temptation comes in different shapes, sizes, colors, and designs. One thing is certain, temptation will come. It's simply just a matter of time.

Perfectly Normal Desires for the Wrong Time

Recently I found myself in a situation which required making a significant decision. The Lord used it to teach me more about temptation. My situation wasn't the typical scenario that most would think of; nonetheless, the principles were the same. Temptation may not always present itself in the obvious manner. We may have perfectly normal desires for the wrong period of time.

Let me explain using a recent chain of events in my life. As mentioned in chapter one, just a few months ago I found myself without a job. Within the first couple of weeks, while I was trying to decompress from the stressful situation, I received a phone call from a recruiter looking to fill a position locally. My first thought was, "Wow, this is great, that was quick Lord, thank you!" I agreed to a phone interview with the global director which would take place the next day.

During the interview I realized my experience was not relevant to the position he was trying to fill. Later I received a call from the recruiter who confirmed my thoughts. I was somewhat relieved as I didn't feel right about the company or the position that I was interviewing for. I agreed to the interview as I wanted to test the waters, and make sure this wasn't in God's plans for me.

Six weeks later, the same recruiter called me again regarding the same position. He indicated that the director, who I previously spoke with was going to be in the local area and wanted to conduct a face to face interview with me. Again, not wanting to miss out on God's plan, I agreed to the in-person interview. The interview was scheduled to take place the next week, following the Women of Faith conference weekend.

The meeting went well. The director indicated that he wanted to meet with me as he felt my background and relationships with the customer would be very advantageous for his company. During our conversation, he aligned the expectations of the position, clearly presenting his needs. As I walked out to the parking lot, I prayed, "Lord, if this is where you are placing me, I will go."

Within an hour after leaving the interview, I received a phone call from the recruiter. He indicated that they were trying to close the deal, and expected the formal offer to come shortly. Another phone call indicated that they would need to overnight the hiring package, and said to expect it around 9am the next day. Immediately I began thinking to myself, "I haven't received a formal offer, nor have I accepted it."

Later that evening, while visiting with some friends, phone calls started coming in. Checking voice mails at 8:30pm, I learned that the director wanted to speak with me immediately. I politely returned his phone call and found myself in a very uncomfortable conversation. The discussion was not consistent with our meeting earlier in the day. He indicated that I would need to report to him the next afternoon to start immediately, if I was willing to accept his new conditions and expectations. The peace that I experienced earlier was completely gone, and I found myself in gut wrenching agony regarding the entire situation.

I was torn between the realization of how much we needed the salary, and the fact that I did not feel God in this decision at all. My husband tried to console me, as I was crying out of control. I didn't know what to do, I had to follow God's Will, regardless of the cost. Eric later indicated that it was heart wrenching to see the look of terror on my face. That is exactly how I felt, complete terror following the phone call. We prayed about the decision, and sought God's direction. Eric assured me that I would know what to do when I woke up the next morning.

The morning hours came and still there was no peace to be found. Once again I found myself in tears, sobbing uncontrollably. I called my mother and explained the situation to her, telling her that I didn't know what to do. The salary was not quite what I was making, but was still very good; however, the position was not for me. My mother gave me sound advice. She told me to just start worshipping and singing to the Lord, and my answer would come. I did just as she told me to do, pouring my heart out to God, praising Him, thanking Him, and worshipping Him for He is worthy.

After spending time in His presence, the Holy Spirit directed me to Matthew chapter 4, the temptation of Jesus Christ. I asked God if I was being tempted. I told Him that I did not understand how this was considered temptation. God showed me that temptation doesn't always come in the obvious manners. At times, temptation disguises itself using different masks. God confirmed that I was being tempted and I needed to trust Him.

Satan knew the plans that God had for me. He knew that I had planned to begin writing this book the very day all of this happened. If you are wondering how Satan would know this, it is because I spend a lot of time talking with God out loud when I am home alone during the day. Satan is the ruler of the kingdom of the air, as mentioned in Ephesians 2:2, and has a serious eavesdropping problem.

After spending time with God, and understanding what I was going through, the answer was clear. I knew what I had to do. I reached out to the recruiter and shared with him my experience from the day before. I told him that the opportunity did not change, the director was still looking for the same skill set as before. Therefore, I was not the person for this job. The conversation went well, and God took care of the details. I had complete peace, once again, even without a paycheck.

Sometimes Satan comes in to offer a solution that is a quick fix, the complete opposite of God's plan for your life. Satan tempts us with quick relief or a resolution to a situation. He tries to convince us to make something happen for the wrong reason or at the wrong time. Taking immediate action may not be completely wrong in itself. However, it may not be what is in God's plan for you at that time. Satan often comes in to distract you from what God has called you to do.

Temptation always finds us when we are the most vulnerable. Whether we are weary, tired, under pressure, looking for a quick fix to relieve our situation, lonely, or have an extreme case of the blues. Temptation will find its way into our lives at the most inopportune moment. As humans we find ourselves tempted within our desires, physical needs, pride, possessions, authority, salary grade, or status in society.

Temptation always seems to find our weakest link, testing us in areas where we are most vulnerable. Think about the story of Solomon in 1 Kings, chapter 11. Solomon had many wives whom he loved and wanted to please. Solomon served the one true God while his wives served other gods. He was pressured into idolatry by his vulnerability and desire to please his wives. His wisdom offered no exemption for Satan's tactics.

Gradually giving into temptation, placing ourselves in situations that are wrong, and making compromises leads us to the place where everything begins to look the same. We no longer see the problem because we have placed ourselves right in the middle of the problem. A chain is only as strong as its weakest link. When we try to tackle life's temptations through our own effort (the weakest link), we often make decisions that will compromise our faith. Without God, the temptation may be too great to overcome. Sometimes we literally must run away from it, just like Joseph did when Potiphar's wife continued to make advances at him. (Genesis 39:10-15)

Entertaining temptation today, creates sin for tomorrow. As humans, we tend to rationalize situations, making them seem more acceptable. We attempt to arrive at a logical conclusion, only to find ourselves doubting what we know. The minute we begin to doubt our values, faith, convictions, or relationship with God we give Satan the ability to move in for his attack. When doubt and temptation set in, we must immediately seek God and dive head first into His Word for answers.

> "You will seek me and find me when you seek me with all of your heart." (Jeremiah 20:13)

Resisting Temptation

So we understand that temptation may come wearing many masks. The question is, how can we resist the temptation immediately so that we do not compromise our faith or relationship with God?

First we must flee, resist, and run from the feeling, person or object that we are being tempted by. Resist the people, places or things that may tempt us in the future. Pray for God to strengthen us in this weakness.

Secondly, we must understand that the temptation may be caused by a desire or need that is unfulfilled in our lives. We need to determine the underlying *root cause* that continues to distract and tempt us. Once we have done this, we need to get into God's Word and seek His direction to overcome it.

Thirdly, looking for another believer in whom you can confide in. Ask them to pray with you regarding this struggle. Reaching out to another believer will not only give you strength through the power of prayer, but will also make you accountable and committed to resisting and overcoming this temptation.

Most importantly, chose the action that will most honor God. God does not lead us into times of temptation. However, there are times when God will allow us to be tempted by Satan. God uses these situations as a proving ground for our faith.

Because we know that temptation will come, we must be ready for it. We must seek the author and finisher of our faith, remember our convictions, and seek the answers in God's Word if we are to hold up under the pressure. Jesus told his disciples: "Pray that you will not fall into temptation," as he walked away into the garden to pray. Jesus was telling His disciples that they would be tempted, some that very evening. (Luke 22:40)

It will happen to you. Be Strong in the Lord. Seek His knowledge, Will and purpose for your life.

Chapter Five

Be Available and Willing

"For I know the plans I have for you," declares the Lord, "plans to prosper you and not to harm you, plans to give you hope and a future. Then you will call upon me and come and pray to me, and I will listen to you. You will seek me and find me when you seek me with all your heart." (Jeremiah 29:11-13)

God has a purpose for each and every one of us. He continually reminds us of this throughout the pages of His Word, the Bible. Sometimes it is not always easy to connect the dots in your life. If you are like me, I want to see the entire picture, not dot by dot.

During my childhood school years I could connect the dots quicker than anyone in my class. I had the desire to know exactly what I was looking at and dealing with. As an adult, I find abstract art a complete frustration. I don't want to think about it, wait to figure it out, or analyze the artwork to understand its purpose. I want it to be obvious.

Sometimes seeking God's purpose in your life is heart wrenching. It's easy to become frustrated when things are not as obvious as you would like them to be. Sometimes you may even question if God has a plan for you. The answer is yes, He does.

Seek God

My husband and I have spent the past two years seeking God in regards to our music ministry. God has placed such an anointing on our music. He has given us an amazing blend that without effort, happens every time. Most vocalists work very hard to achieve this without God. In our hearts we are so willing to serve God and are so ready for His direction. My husband is pretty certain that the bus will be showing up soon. He still awaits a call from the southern gospel touring show.

During our evening conversations we have talked to great lengths regarding next steps, how to *launch* our ministry, etc. Often times we find ourselves discouraged, growing weary, uncertain how long we will have to wait for our answer.

I shared with Eric my desire to get back into ministering with a praise and worship team. I believed that the Lord was wanting us to begin preparing ourselves for a complete line of music ministry. Eric, on the other hand, felt completely different about joining the praise team. He loves to worship the Lord, but didn't feel that we should join a team. He committed to praying about it and seeking God for direction, but was pretty certain the bus would arrive to pick us up before God placed us in a praise and worship ministry.

Months later we found ourselves at dinner with the pastor and his wife asking what we could do to help them with the music ministry of the church. We talked about joining a praise team and several other opportunities. It was five months before anything was implemented, and Eric found it difficult to believe this was in God's plan. During the months of waiting, we continued working on our music, ministering with specials, and seeking the Lord. One evening, walking into church, we were asked to lead worship while the pastoral staff was at a conference. During that service, Eric realized that God was calling us into more than we could begin to imagine. We are still waiting on the bus; however, God is using us where He has planted us for the time being.

I am definitely not a subject matter expert on discerning God's purpose and will for one's life. I struggle with this on a daily basis myself. I have come to understand that when you diligently seek God in prayer and worship and surrender your life to His will, you will hear His voice guiding you. He will guide you every step of the way.

Ellen Vanda

Step Out of your Comfort Zone

At times God may ask you to step out of your comfort zone to serve Him. You may be stretched in areas that you would have never thought was possible. For me, I knew my calling was always in music ministry. I never dreamed of writing a book, or having a ministry of encouragement. But God, had a different plan.

Before surrendering to God, Eric was writing music for the secular world of rock. He sang in bands, recorded a few songs and always wanted to be a rock star. After giving in to God's purpose and calling for his life, his heart is in ministry. Eric has given himself completely to the will of God, whether it is in music, praise and worship or reaching the lost. However, he is still waiting on the bus.

Give God Your Availability, Not Your Limitations

If you want to be used by God, you need to give Him your availability, not your limitations. You need to be ready and willing to answer as Isaiah did in chapter six, "Here I am, send me".

I am thankful that God is so much greater than my thoughts and understanding. He sees beyond my simple desires and gives me so much more. He acknowledges my limitations and uses them as opportunities for growth, because I am willing and available to serve Him.

Being completely honest, there are days when I cannot think beyond my morning shower, the next meeting or appointment. I become needy, distracted and completely frustrated. *But God* has a plan and a purpose for my life. And, He has the same for you.

In Ecclesiastes we read about King Solomon, the wisest man who ever lived in the Bible. Solomon teaches us that living a life without God and His purpose is absolutely meaningless. If we seek to find meaning in our lives through knowledge, money, pleasure, work or social status we will live within our limitations. Living within our limitations deprives us of the blessings and benefits found in God's plan and purpose.

The story of Esther is a clear example of how God uses situations and circumstances that He places His children in for His purpose and glory. Because of Esther's courage and faith in God, she was able to save her people, the Jews, from inhalation at the hands of Haman. Her story is found in the short chapter of Esther, and is full of drama and surprises. It is a definite must read when you feel that you are not understanding God's purpose for your life.

God's Timing

In the story of Esther we learn about the value of waiting for God's perfect timing. For me, waiting on God is challenging. I find myself resisting the desire to make things happen on my own. If Esther chose not to wait on God's timing, the story of Mordecai and Haman's destiny would have ended differently. The results may have led to the inhalation of God's chosen people.

God's timing is always perfect. At times, this may be hard to accept. When we begin to doubt His timing, we become discouraged, frustrated, rebellious and depressed. Psalm 130:5 is a great verse to read when we find waiting to be difficult. It gives us hope in God. Below I have included several translations for this simple verse.

> I am counting on the Lord; yes, I am counting on him. I have put my hope in his word. (NLT)

> I wait for the Lord, my soul waits, and in his word I put my hope. (NIV)

> I pray to God – my life a prayer- And wait for what he'll say and do. My life's on the line before God, my Lord, Waiting and watching till morning, Waiting and watching till morning. (MSG)

Waiting can be a blessing in disguise. God often uses times of waiting to complete a work that He is doing in your life.

Waiting allows you to become more proficient in your faith. As you practice a skill or trade, you gradually get better at it.

Waiting enables you to be prepared for the answers and direction that God is going to give you. Preparing your heart to receive God's direction may sometimes mean sacrificing your own agenda.

Waiting brings greater victory when the answer arrives. It will make you more confident in your faith and perseverance.

Waiting displays the sovereignty of God Almighty. He designs your life, direction, and purpose to give glory to His name.

Be encouraged as you wait for God's direction and purpose in your life. God always shows up just in time and He is there to comfort you as you wait on Him. His ways are not our ways, often His timing seems foreign to us. God sees you where you are. He knows the person He created you to be and has placed so much more in you than you can begin to imagine.

God's Grace may be found in "Plan Be"

Have you ever made a wrong turn in your life trying to follow God's plan, only to find out that it wasn't God's plan at all. Somehow, lost among all the details, you failed to follow the outline. Perhaps you were not given a syllabus outlining the expectations of your journey. You find yourself desolate on the road of life, heading in the wrong direction, with no clue how to get turned around. Unfortunately, I have been there more than once. I am so thankful for God's grace that can be found in "Plan Be". *Be who God has called you to be.*

God uses our bad decisions to teach us His way

In chapter four I shared the story about facing temptation when I started to write this book. If you recall, I had an interview with a company who offered a *quick fix* to my unemployment situation. I soon discovered that it was a distraction to what God wanted me to do at that time in my life. A temptation, which offered quick relief, that came with a big price tag. Continuing with that story, I want to share with you something that God placed on my heart several days later.

I was driving down the road, thinking of what I needed to get done that day, and I heard God say, "I never meant for you to be at *former company*. It was never My will for you to go through what you went through." Talk about something sending you to your knees. I had to pull over, put myself together, wipe the tears away and catch my breath. As I began to pray, thanking God for His provision, He revealed more to me.

God told me that He allowed the second lesson to come around to see if I truly wanted His will for my life, or if I would once again accept a *quick fix*. I knew He was referring to the job that I had interviewed for. In that moment, I knew my actions had pleased the Lord. I found favor by seeking Him in my decision and glorifying His name with my obedience. I will never forget that day, the lesson, and knowing that something I did pleased God.

That was truly a WOW moment with my God. Let me put this all into perspective. Don't you find yourself frustrated with the movies that show you the ending moments, only to jump you back to weeks, months or years before.

A year earlier, I was working as a Program Manager for a company that I had been with for many years, servicing a large corporate customer. That company eventually lost the account, becoming only a supplier instead of a service provider, and our roles changed significantly. I recognized that it was time for a change in my career, but hesitated to move as I loved the company.

One day I received a call from a corporate recruiter, from another company, who recently aligned themselves to service this same customer. They were looking for an Account Manager who could open an office, build a local team and grow the business as they were new to the area. The call came in on a Friday, as my work week was coming to an end. After spending an hour on the phone interview, the recruiter asked if I would be willing to speak with the CEO of the company on Monday.

My husband and I researched the company as much as we could, prayed about it and felt that it had to be from God as it landed right in my lap. We thought it was time to move on and God was making things easy for us.

The conversation took place on Monday, it was definitely not the typical interview that I was expecting. The CEO and I hit it off amazingly well, used the same terminology of the industry, and found that we had colleagues in common. He offered me the position with $16,000/year pay increase, along with additional commission compensation. I immediately accepted, called my husband and told him of the news. I tendered my resignation the next day, offering a two week notice.

I spent the next year working long hours, building the business and team, while reporting to a voice on the phone. It was the most stressful year of my career. The corporation had zero procedures in place for their customers, offices and staff members. Corporate protocol included flying by the seat of their pants for most decisions. The CEO's demeanor, decisions and leadership was up and down like a roller coaster.

I found myself spending my evenings and weekends working from home. Most evenings I would spend time crying in my husband's arms, trying to find the strength to face another day. I had to be strong for my team, offering leadership, guidance, and putting together processes and procedures for our team to follow.

I prayed on my way to work, asking God to go before me. I prayed all the way home, thanking God for getting me through another day. At times during the day, I would cry out to God for guidance, peace, and comfort.

After almost a year of this, I finally met someone from the company. The corporate recruiter who found me also traveled to Peoria to end my employment. The rest of the story was mentioned in the beginning of this book.

Back to my story.

"I never meant for you to be at *former company.* It was never My will for you to go through what you went through."

Accepting this job was never in God's plan for my life. The job happened very quickly, effortlessly, offering a *quick fix* to the career dilemma I was facing. It came with an attractive salary and bonus. It was never part of God's plan for my life. There were times that he used the lemon that I chose to make lemonade, there were even times He used me to minister to my team.

But God never intended for me to go through everything I chose to go through. I made the wrong turn, the wrong decision and lost my way. *But God* never forsake me, He never turned away. He was always with me, even in the darkest of days. We made lemonade until He freed me from it all.

If this isn't enough in itself, it doesn't end here. God also revealed to me that He brought the same situation around again to see if I would make the same decision again. Would I accept a quick fix and financial relief over His purpose and plan for my life? I am pleased to say that I got it right the second time around. Praise the Lord! I am determined to follow God's lead and direction for my life.

After taking all of this in, and spending time with God, this is what I told Him. "God, your grace and mercy is in *Plan Be* and I am so thankful that you never let go of me." I am absolutely overwhelmed and amazed by His love and will continue to be every day of my life.

Chapter Six

Turn Down the Noise

Do you remember the family television shows of the 70's and 80's? I wish our lives today could be as simple as they were so many years ago. People believed in hard work. They were committed to their families and most importantly, served the Lord fervently. I remember my childhood and adolescent years, life was so much easier for everyone then. My parents struggled at times, but nothing like families struggle today. Life has changed.

Christians throughout the generations have something that has never changed, our God. His principles for living the Christian life are still clearly stated in His Holy Word, the Bible. God's morals, values and ethics have not swayed. He has not changed His mind. He is constant, consistent and faithful according to His Word. God is still the same yesterday, today and will be tomorrow. The change has obviously been imposed by today's society.

Our lives are so technically advanced, so modernized, so busy and crammed full of "stuff" that we sometimes forget to align our priorities with God's Will. Parents are conforming to society's expectations by enrolling their children in all types of sports, music programs, dance programs, church programs and private lessons. Someone needs to create a "Day Timer" designed exclusively for children and their busy lifestyles. Adults are trying to keep up with society's expectations for their career, education, children, lifestyle and marriage. Churches have become pawns in the entertainment business, gearing services to be more "user friendly" and less Bible focused as not to offend anyone. Many church services have been shortened to accommodate their member's busy lifestyles, and Sunday evening services are very seldom heard of. We are too busy for our own good. Our lifestyles are becoming a distraction from our purpose as Christians.

We have cell phones that are permanently attached to us, only water can separate us from our phones. Unfortunately, we have equipped our young children with the same curse. We cannot go out to eat without checking in on our social network, or catching a look at our emails while talking with our family. I encourage you to take a minute to look around during your next restaurant adventure, notice the couples who are dining together. They never talk with each other. They are too busy texting and socializing in the media world. Families no longer talk, the kids are glued to their cell phones or video games. Husband and wives talk more to their friends on Facebook than they do each other.

I am convinced that the changes in our society and world today are a direct result of Satan's war strategies. His tactical playbook may look something like this.

Husbands and Wives

> ➢ Introduce them to the Jones family, teach them to covet their neighbor's stuff. They will spend their lives trying to make more money to buy more stuff.
> ➢ Keep the wives busy running their children to every event, game, lesson, store, play date and party to eliminate the time that they would spend with God.
> ➢ Teach the parents how to utilize the "electronic babysitter" of choice. This will eventually isolate the children from their parents.
> ➢ Keep the married couple always wanting, needing, and desiring more. This will eventually put a wedge in their relationship. Busy schedules and more demands will no longer afford the opportunity for their needs to be fulfilled.
> ➢ Introduce the corporate ladder, every wrung leads to more hunger and desire.
> ➢ Introduce the social media, an instant cure for loneliness and isolation.

Families

> ➢ Introduce the Family Talk and Text Plan from their local cellular provider. Provide free phones for every member of the family so they are available to text and talk during all hours of the night. Be sure to provide them with unlimited internet service. The internet can offer things beyond their imagination and with limited parental control.
>
> ➢ Introduce DVR, satellite television and hundreds of channels to consume the hours the family would normally spend time together. Note, they aren't talking while they are watching shows, which will break down communication.
>
> ➢ Be sure to eliminate family bonding activities, giving each member of the family a desire for independence. Provide them with endless choices to keep everyone running in different directions.

Teenagers

> ➢ Take advantage of insecurities, curiosities, rebellion, hormonal changes and desires.
>
> ➢ Isolate the teenagers from their parents. The divide and conquer concept always works.
>
> ➢ Remind them that texting and talking on their cell phones throughout the night gives them the privacy

that they long for. Privacy to explore conversations they shouldn't be having. Internet access on their phones offers them complete freedom without parental control.

➢ Introduce them to alcohol, drugs and sex to fulfill the emptiness in their busy lifestyles.

➢ Remind them that going to church is not the favorable trend.

Society

➢ Convince them that Satan doesn't exist. This is the most successful lie that you can tell them. It will change everything!

➢ Divide, conquer, destroy, wage war, kill innocent lives, and create new religions and Gods for society to follow.

➢ Infiltrate the world with NOISE. So much noise that people can no longer hear God and the Holy Spirit. Your worries will be over.

➢ Introduce new idols for people to serve including fitness, designer brands, fast cars, and high paying careers.

➢ Keep everyone so busy that they no longer have time to invest in the Kingdom of God.

➢ Change Christmas
   1. No longer allow "Merry Christmas" to be used, Happy Holidays is much more appropriate.
   2. No longer allow employers to display Christmas trees, it may offend other religions.

3. Keep businesses open so employees have to work.
4. Make it more about the gifts, presents, movies, songs, and euphoria than about the Christ child and virgin birth.

➤ Take God out of the schools, courtrooms, places of employment, ceremonies and government. Without God's involvement, chaos is certain to follow.

Churches

➤ Introduce the concept of being a "user friendly" church.

➤ Teach them that by preaching the word of God, folks may be offended and retract their financial support.

➤ Convince them to remove the cross from their churches. Visitors may find it offensive.

➤ Introduce compromise to the leaders of the church.

➤ Attack the unity of the body. Bring division among the congregation.

➤ Bring jealousy into the house of God. It will slowly destroy ministries, relationships and leadership.

➤ Let the Spirit of Division walk the isles.

➤ Make sure the musicians, vocalists and praise teams all have such self-serving ego's that there will be no chance they can become unified to usher in the presence of God.

➤ Keep the youth services dark, it teaches them to hide their religion so no one knows they serve God.

Reading through this list is somewhat entertaining until you sit back and take inventory of what is happening in your life, home, family, church and society. So many times Christians forget that there is an enemy named Satan who is out to destroy lives, churches and most importantly, families. His time on earth is limited, so his attacks are more intense than they have ever been. His biggest tactic is to keep Christians so busy in their lives that they no longer find time to spend with God. He places so much noise in our lives that we can no longer hear the *Still Small Voice* speaking to our hearts and soul. The voice of God and the Holy Spirit.

It is time for Christians to evaluate their priorities and values, and take control of their lives. We need to find more time on our knees than in our cars. We need to turn off the television and open the Word of God. We need to spend time in prayer as husbands and wives, families, and churches. We need to begin investing our time, resources and lives in the Kingdom of God. Time is running out. The world is spiraling out of control, and people are looking for answers. We know the truth they are seeking. We know the source for the unconditional love they are lacking in their lives. We know the one way to eternal life, salvation through Jesus Christ. We must decrease so the Spirit of God can increase in our lives, relationships, families and churches. Make this your prayer today, make it your heart's cry.

He must become greater; I must become less. (John 3:30)

John the Baptist's life was purposed to direct people to God until the Son of God appeared on the banks of the Jordan River. When he met Jesus, John knew his purpose had been fulfilled. He needed to become less so that Jesus Christ could become greater. His life became a megaphone pointing people to the Son of the Living God. Is your life directing people to Jesus? Are you living a life that has others questioning why you are so joyful, fulfilled, and complete? He must become greater, and our priorities need to be realigned.

Can you hear God's voice through the noise in your life?

Recently I was walking in the Chicago Loop around 4pm during the week. I struggled to hear myself think, as I tried to find the address of where I needed to be. The noise of the city was overwhelming. People talking, cell phones on speaker, protestors screaming out their opposition, cars sounding their horns, tires screeching to halts, people yelling out for taxis, and air brakes puffing from buses approaching intersections. I couldn't help but notice that even the beautiful fountains added to the symphony of noise, the water slapping violently in the wind.

As Christians, we need to eliminate the unnecessary noise in our lives. The noise that drowns out the voice of God. I challenge you to begin hearing the noise that is consuming your life. Chose a typical day to make your observations. At the end of the day, write down your experiences and spend time reflecting on the noise that can be eliminated from your life. I understand the noise of the city, while walking down the sidewalk, cannot be eliminated. However, you will begin noticing what noise is drowning out the "Still Small Voice" of your Creator.

I have to be honest, I wasn't always aware of the noise in my life. I went about life the same way everyone else does, experiencing the hustle and stress of the corporate world while trying to juggle my family responsibilities. When my body finally had all the noise it could take, I found myself eating stomach relievers and taking high blood pressure medication. In the evenings I would spend time in complete silence just to get away from it all. Some evenings I couldn't hold back the tears, life had become too difficult. It was then I knew something had to change.

I recall one specific day when I had reached my breaking point. After work I rushed out to get into my car before anyone caught a glimpse of me crying. I found myself so overwhelmed from a job that I once loved. After having a rough evening, I decided to take a sick day for the next morning. Using an allotted sick day is something that I very seldom do. Normally, a day when I was not feeling well, fighting a cold or the flu, I would work from home. Usually working longer than eight hours.

The next day, I got up with my husband as he left for work. I sent out a few emails, aligned the resources for the team, gave everyone the heads up that I was taking a sick day and then put my "out of office" on my email. I turned off my cell phone, unplugged my laptop and refrained from turning on the television, radio or any household appliance. I promised myself that I would not perform any type of work, even household chores. I simply needed the noise to stop.

Being the water lover that I am, I took a walk around the lagoon in the park. I also walked down along the river banks. I was desperately looking for answers, needing to find balance and desiring to hear the voice of God. At times I found myself with tears running down my face as I cried out to God, singing songs of worship to Him. God met me where I was at, in the condition I was in and showered me with His amazing grace. He picked me up and put me back in the game. We serve a loving, faithful God that will never forsake us in our desperation.

On that day, I realized I had to eliminate the noise from my life. It was time to realign my priorities and spend more time in His presence. That day completely changed my home and work life. Most importantly, it changed my walk with the Lord.

The Noise from Your Past

As women, we are always reflecting on our lives. A lot of us have things in our past that seem to find their way out of our sub-conscious at one time or another. Baggage that checks itself out of the claim department and shows up on your doorstep at the most inopportune moments. I am here to encourage you to release yourself from the baggage of the past and remove that noise from your life. You are well aware of the noise I am referring to. The noise that comes to steal your joy, rob your self-worth and shake the ground you are standing on. This noise doesn't come from God, it comes from Satan. The enemy likes to remind of us our former lives, sins and failures because it deters us from moving forward.

> Brothers, I do not consider myself yet to have taken hold of it. But one thing I do: Forgetting what is behind and straining toward what is ahead. I press on toward the goal to win the prize for which God has called me heavenward in Christ Jesus. (Philippians 3:13-14)

Paul had a lot of baggage that he carried around with him throughout his life, until he met his Savior, Jesus Christ. Paul had plenty to be ashamed about, he persecuted and killed many of God's children while he was known as Saul. *But God* gave him a new name, and a new song to sing. Paul spent his time and energy running the race that God placed in front of him. The race was not behind him.

When we place our hope in Christ, we need to let go of all the baggage that has followed us around. Some of us even have it strapped together to enable us to transport it easier, a train of baggage dragging behind us. Let it go. Give it to God, and begin running the race that He has placed in front of you! Eliminate the noise of your past and begin listening to the voice of your future, God's voice.

As Christians we need to equip our lives with a noise filter, similar to the air filters that we purchase for our homes. We need to periodically change the filter to ensure that the useless noise in our lives is being extracted. We live in a society that will always create noise.

With God's help we are able to identify areas in our lives that creates unproductive noise. We need to filter it out so that we will not miss anything that God may be wanting to say to us. I don't know about you, but I don't want to miss out with God. Noise is not going to get in my way!

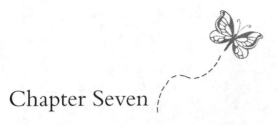

Chapter Seven

Created to Worship

When God formed us in our mother's womb He placed a desire in us, the innate desire to worship. As we look at the human race from the beginning of time, the need and desire to worship has always been present. In Genesis we read about Adam and Eve walking with God in the garden daily. They spent time with Him, talked with Him and offered their praise and gratefulness to the Lord for His provision.

The pages of the Old Testament clearly illustrate that men and women had the need to worship something or someone. God's children worshipped Him, offering sacrifices for atonement of their sins. However, others chose to worship other gods, even golden idols.

Today, the people of the world still have the desire to worship. Some worship God Almighty, the Alpha and Omega, the Beginning and the End, the Creator, the one true God. While others worship the gods of other religions, idols in their own lives, even some of the Hollywood stars. God created us to be worshippers for His Glory.

In John chapter 4, Jesus meets a Samaritan woman at Jacob's Well in Samaria. He asks the woman for a drink and uses this opportunity to teach her about drinking from the well of living water. During their conversation, the Samaritan woman explains that they worship on this mountain, as their fathers did. Jesus then teaches her about true worship.

> Believe me, woman, a time is coming when you will worship the Father neither on this mountain nor in Jerusalem. You Samaritans worship what you do not know, we worship what we do know, for salvation is here from the Jews. Yet a time is coming and has now come when the true worshipers will worship the Father in spirit and truth, for they are the kind of worshipers the Father seeks. God is spirit, and his worshipers must worship in spirit and in truth. (John 4: 21-24)

I have also included a paraphrased scripture from *The Voice* that I feel offers a significant perspective regarding worship.

> Woman, I tell you that neither *is so*. Believe this: a new day is coming—in fact, it's already here—when the importance will not be placed on the time and place of worship but on the truthful hearts of worshipers. You worship what you don't know while we worship what

we do know, for God's salvation is coming through the Jews. The Father is spirit, and He is seeking followers whose worship is sourced in truth and deeply spiritual as well. Regardless of whether you are in Jerusalem or on this mountain, if you do not seek the Father, then you do not worship. (John 4: 21-24 Voice)

How Do We Praise and Worship Our God?

Worship is a natural behavior when you have an intimate relationship with God and His Son, Jesus Christ. The more time you spend in His presence, the more you will understand Him. The more you understand Him, the more thankful you will be for what He is doing in your life. When your heart becomes full of gratitude, you will want to praise and worship Him.

This is how I define praise and worship. "An outwardly reaction to my innermost feelings of gratitude, reverence, appreciation, respect, amazement, and joy for my Creator the Lord God Almighty and His Son, the Savior of my soul, Jesus Christ."

For me, praise and worship is lifting my voice in song, my hands in surrender, and the deepest part of me, my heart and soul, in praise for He who is and what He has done. I find myself worshipping the Lord throughout my day; thanking Him, singing to Him, seeking Him and always finding Him.

I sing praises to His name silently when I go to sleep, and it always amazes me to find His praise on my lips when I awake. It may be one of the latest praise and worship songs, a hymn, or something I really need for that day. I hear the sweet voice of God singing back to me to start my day. What better way could there possibly be than to start your day hearing your heavenly Father singing over you. Zephaniah must have experienced this as well encouraging him to write in his book of the Bible.

> The Lord your God is with you, He is mighty to save. He will take great delight in you, He will quiet you with his love, He will rejoice over you with singing. (Zephaniah 3:17)

Praise and worship will help you build an intimate relationship with God and His Son, Jesus Christ. The closer your relationship becomes with the Lord, the more you will want to sing His praises and worship His name. The more you seek His face, the more you will find yourself in His presence. The more you are in His presence, the more you will want to worship Him. It is all so very simple.

If you have never taken the time to enter into His presence before, today is the day. There is power beyond anything you can imagine. Peace beyond comprehension. Joy that is overflowing. There is forgiveness for anything that you have ever done, just ask for it. You will find understanding, grace, mercy and unending love. There is nothing this world can offer you that can compares to the unconditional love God has for you.

In Psalm 103 David instructs us to give God praise for the things He is doing in our lives. David writes so much about singing to the Lord, praising His name, playing musical instruments and dancing unto the Lord in Psalms. I challenge you to spend time in the book of Psalms every day, reading a few verses or chapter. It is encouraging, uplifting, soothing, and teaches you how to worship the Lord.

What Will Praise and Worship Do For Us?

Spending time praising and worshipping the Lord will change your life. Your mind will begin to focus on God instead of your problems, failures, past, and inadequacies. You will start to focus on God's majesty, power, grace, mercy, love, faithfulness and forgiveness.

When I spend time in praise and worship with God I find my attitude is adjusted, my priorities are realigned, and my soul is at peace. We were created to worship God. He placed a hunger and thirst in our souls for intimacy with Him.

If you do not have this unquenchable desire to praise and worship Him, start asking God to place this in your heart. There is nothing wrong with asking God to draw you closer to Him; to place an unquenchable thirst in your soul for more intimacy with Him; and to have a better understanding of who He is. If you are feeling lost, lonely, or feel that you have something missing inside of you, start lifting your voice to God. Begin to thank Him for who He is. Ask Him to draw close to you and teach you His ways. He will meet you where you are, and take you to where He wants you to be. I promise.

Praising God through the Storms of Life

In Acts chapter 16, we read about Paul and Silas who were stripped and beaten, placed in stocks around their feet, and thrown into a prison for being servants of God. At the midnight hour, when things were looking very grim and their bodies were crying out in pain, Paul and Silas began singing praises to God. Can you imagine what the other prisoners were thinking? It's the middle of the night, two men who were badly beaten, bound in chains, sitting up as much as they could in efforts to lift their voices to the Lord Most High. Paul and Silas, reaching out from their circumstances to enter the presence of the Lord.

No matter what circumstances you may be facing, reach out beyond your pain, hurt, insecurities, doubt and begin praising the Lord. In Psalm 30:11 David wrote, "You turned my wailing into dancing, you removed my sackcloth and clothed me with joy, that my heart may sing to you and not be silent. O Lord my God, I will give you thanks forever."

It is amazing how God changes your heart as you face the storms of your life. Each storm brings soul cleansing rain. Learn to praise Him in the rain, and seek His face. As you begin to worship your Lord, spend time at His feet, in His presence, seeking His face. You will find knowledge and gain understanding of His plans and direction for your life. The storms of life become less threatening when you are sitting at the feet of the Creator of the Universe.

Have you ever stood at the foot of a mountain and realized just how small you really are? During my high school years, my campus youth director shared a story with me that I have never forgotten. He gave me a penny in my hand and asked me to hold it up in front of my eyes. While I was doing that he instructed me to look at the mountain behind the penny. The penny seemed terribly large compared to the mountain in the background. He then instructed me to walk towards the mountain. As I walked toward the mountain, the penny became smaller and the mountain was enormous. Try it, it's amazing.

He explained to me that the penny symbolizes my circumstances or problems, the mountain was to represent God. What he was trying to illustrate to me was the further away from God we are, the greater our problems and circumstances appear. The closer we get to the feet of God, the smaller our problems and circumstances become.

As we begin to storm the gates of heaven with our praise and worship, we will begin to see healing, chains broken, strongholds released, salvation for our family members, and miracles happen.

> I will extol the Lord at all times; his praise will always be on my lips. (Psalm 34:1)

Have a Heart of Worship

True worship is a vehicle that will transport us into to the presence of God. It is in His presence that we will begin to understand His infinite power and grace. In His presence, our lives are transformed.

I encourage you to build your life around praising and worshipping God. Make it a priority. Spending intimate time with God everyday through worship, prayer and reading His word will better prepare you for life.

When you truly meet God, praise and worship will be your only response. We worship Him because He alone is worthy of our praise. Only God can satisfy the hunger and thirst He has placed innately within us. There is nothing that the world can offer us that will ever take His place. We were created to worship Him.

Sunday is right around the corner. As you spend time with the Lord today, begin preparing your heart for your Sunday morning service. Go expecting to receive from God. Prepare your heart to enter into worship *before* Sunday morning. Instead of waiting for God to show up in the church service, bring Him with you to church. Let His praise always be on your lips, and you will never be disappointed. Don't rely on the pastor or praise team to get you pumped up for God. Be pumped up when you walk in the door, and see what amazing things God can do through you!

Conclusion

The Reflection in the Mirror

Becoming the woman that God has called you to be is an exciting adventure. Whether you are beginning the journey for the first time, or have the desire for a more intimate relationship with your Creator, get ready for the most exhilarating experience of your life!

As you begin to seek God's plan and purpose for your life, everything will change. Your priorities, ideals, goals, expectations, and plans will become more aligned with God's purpose and His plan. The more you seek God and spend time in His presence, the more you will begin to understand His Will for your life. It truly will be the greatest adventure you have ever embarked on, a journey that will never end.

God has a purpose for your life, He has had a plan since the day you were conceived. Don't be afraid to step out of your comfort zone, relinquish all fears and give God your availability. Be like Isaiah, "Here I am, send me."

God's timing may not always be aligned with your expectations, His ways are not your ways; however, He will always show up just in time. He will meet you where you are and take you to where He wants you to be. God is a loving and faithful Father who will never leave you or forsake you, even when you feel the world is closing in and your hope is gone.

When you find yourself lost among the bad decisions, actions, behavior and failures of your life, look to God. He is waiting with open arms to take you out of your current circumstances. He will place you in His "Plan Be" where you will find His grace, mercy and forgiveness. God uses your failures, bad decisions, and insufficiencies as opportunities for growth. God will be glorified through your deliverance, restoration and new purpose. When He begins to take your life to new levels, people will begin to notice the change and will want to know more about your Lord, providing you with the opportunity to share what God has done in your life. Tell them what God has given you, brought you through, and delivered you from.

As you embark on the journey to *become* all that God has for you to be, you need to spend time reading the instruction manual in Romans chapter 12. Be joyful in the hope that you have in Jesus Christ, for He has overcome the world. Assess your life on a regular basis to ensure that you are a living example of the "Be Attitudes" that Paul teaches about. Reach out to the hurting, broken and the lost with your time, your love and acceptance. Be a lighthouse, point the lost to Jesus Christ. You never know when the storms of life will toss someone in your path who is shipwrecked and desperately needs to meet the Master of their turbulent sea.

Becoming is simply building a relationship with God that will change your life forever. Your relationships will only be as strong as the effort you put into them. Work on your relationship with your Heavenly Father on a daily basis. He waits, as any parent does, to hear about your day. He wants to know what has given you joy and what is causing you pain. He wants you to ask Him for His blessings and provision, even though He already knows your needs. God wants to be the first priority in your life.

As the world continues to spin violently out of control, you may find your life filled with more noise than ever before. You most likely juggle between your career, family, marriage, children and social schedule on a daily basis. By evening, you try to unwind, hoping to regain the strength to do it all over again tomorrow. In the remaining moments of the evening you feel the tugging at your heart. "I miss my time with you", God says. "Do you have any time left for Me? I've been waiting for you."

You need to re-evaluate your life. Realign your priorities and assess your values. Define the unwanted noise in your life, and make the needed adjustments. It is time to begin living by God's expectations instead of trying to satisfy the never ending desires of the world. Free your family from the world's grasp and get back to the basics with God.

If you struggle with noise from your past, perhaps a haunting voice that tries to pull you backwards, give the battle to God. No longer carry the baggage that weighs you down and hinders you from becoming who God has called you to be. Leave the bags containing your past failures, defeats, sins, hurts and brokenness at the feet of Jesus. Begin living your life forward and never look back. When the enemy tries to send you to the baggage claim department to retrieve your past, tell him that it is covered by the blood of Jesus Christ and has been tossed into the sea. No longer do you have any baggage, bondage, sin, fears, or regrets. The chains have been broken and Jesus Christ has set you free.

You have been given the gift of eternal life through Jesus Christ. Your God, the creator of this world, knew from the beginning of time that you would need a Savior. He sent His Son into the world not to condemn the world, but that through Him the world might be saved (John 3:16-17). This gives you a reason to be overflowing with praise and worship for your Lord.

You were created to worship God in spirit and in truth, becoming a *true* worshiper. When you take time to worship God for who He is and what He has done in your life, you will change. Your attitude will become more aligned with God's principles. Your heart will beat with compassion. You will desire to have true intimacy with Him. Spending time in the presence of God is something beyond what words can possibly describe. I encourage you to begin spending time with Him, your life will never be the same.

Becoming who God has called you to be is a rewarding journey that never ends. Every day as you look in the mirror you will see His reflection of love in your eyes. His joy will make you smile. His glory will be on your countenance. You will understand the rewards of serving our Creator, Our God and His Son, Jesus Christ.

Become more than you ever thought was possible. Let the adventure begin!

Next Steps

Perhaps you have read this book and want to know God and His Son, Jesus Christ personally. You desire a loving relationship with the Creator and Savior of the world. Understand that you have already experienced the first step, the tugging at your heart by the Holy Spirit. God is reaching out to you. He loves you so much that He sent His son to live a sinless life on this earth, and die a horrific death on the cross. Jesus loved you so much that He laid down His life to pay the debt for your sins. He loves you and believes that you are someone really special.

Please say this prayer with me as you make the most important decision of your life….

Dear Heavenly Father,

Thank you for loving me so much that you sent your only Son, Jesus, to die on the cross for my sins. I have felt you tugging at my heart, and I am opening the door for you to come in to my life. I know that I am a sinner, and I ask you to forgive me of my sins. From this day forward, help me to become more like you. Fill my heart with love and compassion for your children.

Help me not to judge but to forgive others. Write the scriptures on my heart as I read your Holy Word. I desire to know you and will seek your face in prayer daily as we walk this journey together. Even when you are quiet, I know you are with me and you will never forsake me, even in my weaknesses.

In Jesus' name I pray this sinner's prayer and by faith I accept your forgiveness. Help me to forgive myself.

Until we talk again……..

Amen

If you have said this prayer and have asked Jesus to come into your life, you are officially on an exciting new adventure. Get plugged in to a Bible based church, cell group, fellowship group, women's group, etc. Start sharing what God is doing in your life. Begin reaching out to others who are hurting and lost. Spend time visiting with God through His Word, the Bible. As you read the pages, His words will penetrate your heart and you will start to know Him in a powerful and amazing way. If something is going right in your day, thank Him for it; if you are struggling, ask Him for help. He desires a close relationship with you and wants to walk with you every day. Always remember, He is only a prayer away.
Congratulations Dear Friend……see you in heaven one day!

The book of Romans tells us about forgiveness for our sins and righteousness through our faith in Jesus Christ.

> But now a righteousness from God, apart from law, has been made known, to which the Law and the Prophets testify. This righteousness from God comes through faith in the Jesus Christ to all who believe. There is no difference, for all have sinned and fall short of the glory of God, and are justified freely by His grace through the redemption that came by Christ Jesus. (Romans 3: 21-24)

> For the wages of sin is death, but the gift of God is eternal life in Christ Jesus our Lord. (Romans 6:23)

> Everyone who calls on the name of the Lord will be saved. (Romans 10:13)

If you have ever doubted that God loves you, read the book of John in the New Testament of the Bible.

> For God so loved the world that he gave his one and only Son, that whoever believes in Him shall not perish but have eternal life. For God did not send his Son into the world to condemn the world, but to save the world through him. (John 3:16-17)

As Jesus prayed to His Father in the garden, before he was arrested and sentenced to be crucified on the cross, He prayed for you and me. His prayer is found in John chapter 17.

> Father, the time has come, Glorify your Son, that your Son may glorify you. For you granted Him authority over all people that He might give eternal life to all those you have given Him. Now this is eternal life: that they may know you, the only true God, and Jesus Christ, whom you have sent. I have brought you glory on earth by completing the work gave me to do. And now, Father, glorify me in your presence with the glory I had with you before the world began." (John 17:1-5)